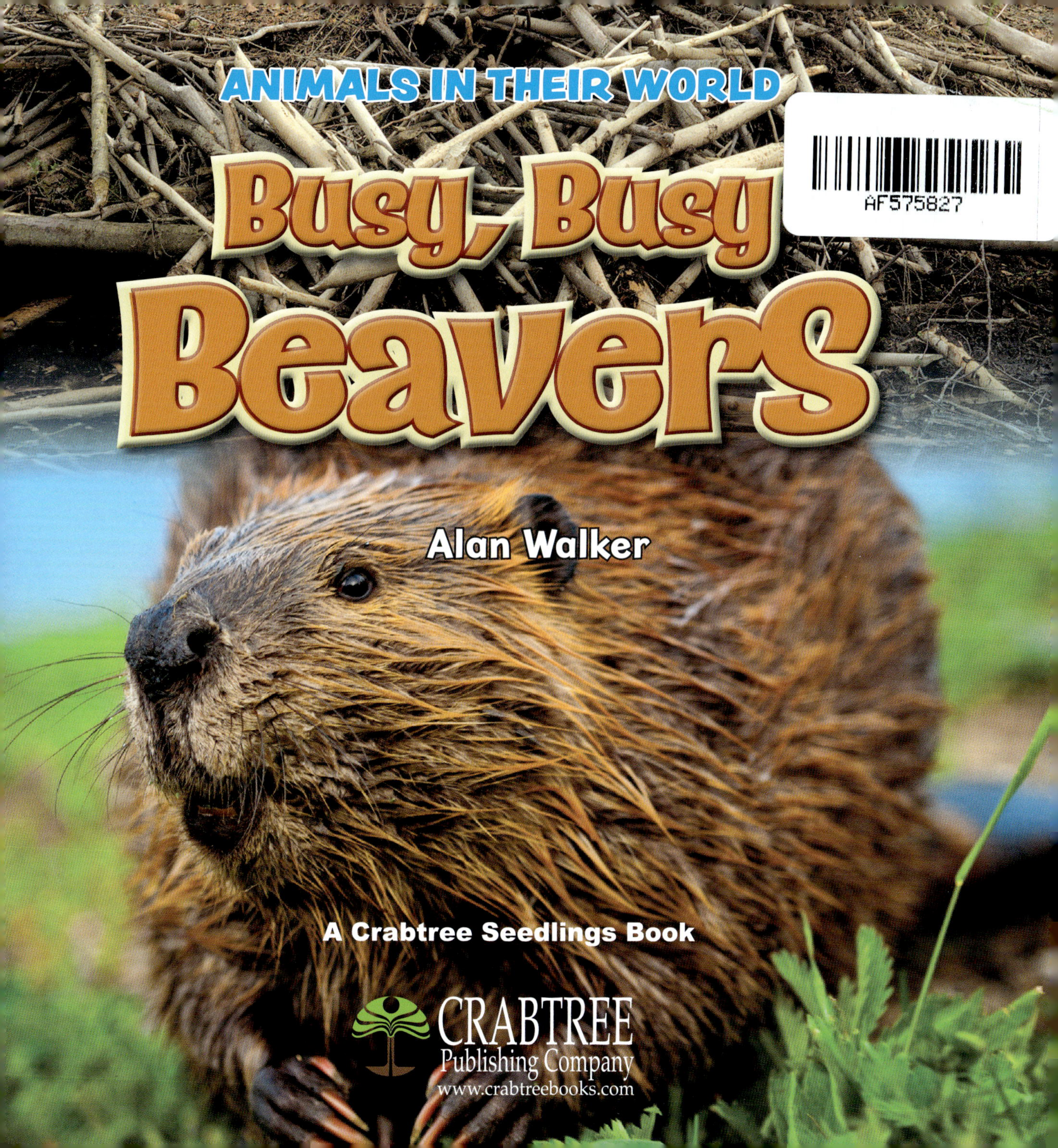
ANIMALS IN THEIR WORLD
Busy, Busy Beavers
Alan Walker
A Crabtree Seedlings Book
CRABTREE
Publishing Company
www.crabtreebooks.com

North American Beaver

Table of Contents

Beavers

Beavers are **herbivores**. They love to eat twigs, leaves, roots, grasses, and berries.

Beavers can be found in forests in North America, Europe, and Asia.

Beavers also love to build. Beavers build **dams**.

Building dams keeps beavers very busy.

beaver skull

Building a Dam

Beavers use their large teeth to chew and **gnaw** through trees and branches.

A beaver can gnaw through a large tree very quickly.

Beavers place mud, cut trees, and branches across a stream. This makes a dam.

The dam stops the water flow and makes a pond.

beaver pond

Beaver Homes

Beaver homes are called **lodges.** Beavers often build their lodges on a beaver pond.

Beaver lodges are made of branches and mud.

beaver lodge

beaver lodge

Lodges provide **shelter** in the cold, winter months. Lodges are also used for storing food.

beaver kit

Baby Beavers

A lodge is a safe place to raise baby beavers. Baby beavers are called kits.

Beavers live in groups called **colonies**. Baby beavers live with their parents for up to three years.

Glossary

colonies (KOL-uh-neez): Colonies are groups of animals that live together.

dams (DAMZ): Dams are built across rivers or streams to stop water flow.

gnaw (NAW): To gnaw is to keep biting on something.

herbivores (HUR-buh-vorz): Herbivores are animals that eat only plants.

lodges (LOJ-iz): Lodges are beaver homes. They are made of branches and mud.

shelter (SHEL-tur): Shelter is a place an animal can live and hide from bad weather and danger.

Index

Help keep areas where beavers build dams and lodges clean and safe.

School-to-Home Support for Caregivers and Teachers

This book helps children grow by letting them practice reading. Here are a few guiding questions to help the reader build his or her comprehension skills. Possible answers appear here in red.

Before Reading

- **What do I think this book is about?** I think this book is about beavers and their habitat. I think this book is about how beavers build their homes.
- **What do I want to learn about this topic?** I want to learn more facts about beavers and their families. I want to learn where I can see beavers in nature.

During Reading

- **I wonder why...** I wonder why beavers have buck teeth. I wonder why beavers build dams.
- **What have I learned so far?** I have learned that beavers eat twigs, leaves, roots, grasses, and berries. I have learned that baby beavers live with their parents for up to three years.

After Reading

- **What details did I learn about this topic?** I have learned that lodges are beaver homes made of branches and mud. I have learned that baby beavers are called kits.
- **Read the book again and look for the glossary words.** I see the word *gnaw* on page 9, and the word *shelter* on page 17. The other glossary words are found on page 22.

Library and Archives Canada Cataloguing in Publication

Available at the Library and Archives Canada

Library of Congress Cataloging-in-Publication Data

Available at the Library of Congress

Crabtree Publishing Company

www.crabtreebooks.com 1–800–387–7650

Print book version produced jointly with Blue Door Education in 2023

Written by: Alan Walker

Print coordinator: Katherine Berti

Printed in the U.S.A./072022/CG20220201

Photo Credits: istock.com, shutterstock.com, Cover: istock.com | kwiktor. P02-03: itosck.com | Anna39. shutterstock.com | Viktor Loki. P04-05: shutterstock.com | Tommy Svensson, shutterstock.com | Marie Dirgova. P06-07: istock.com | aime Espinosa de los Monteros. P08-09: istock.com | MyImages_Micha. shutterstock.com | Audrey Snider-Bell. shutterstock.com | Moonhorn P10-11: shutterstock.com | Cezary Morga, shutterstock.com | Chase Dekker. P12-13: shutterstock | nyker P14-15: istock.com | Bob Hilscher. shutterstock.com | Viktor Loki P16-17: istock.com | SzymonBartosz, istock.com | Matthew_Miller P18-19: istock.com | robertcicchetti. shutterstock.com | Geoffrey Kuchera . P20-21: istock.com | Dan Pepper. shutterstock.com | Piotr Kamionka. P23: shutterstock.com | EZ-Stock Studio.

Published in the United States
Crabtree Publishing
347 Fifth Ave.
Suite 1402-145
New York, NY 10016

Published in Canada
Crabtree Publishing
616 Welland Ave.
St. Catharines, Ontario
L2M 5V6